How to draw MANGA
FANTASY FIGHTERS

Published by Top That! Publishing plc
Tide Mill Way, Woodbridge, Suffolk, IP12 1AP, UK
www.topthatpublishing.com
Copyright © 2012 Top That! Publishing plc
All rights reserved
0 2 4 6 8 9 7 5 3 1
Printed and bound in China

WELCOME TO MANGA

Manga is a style of drawing that started in Japan. In Japanese 'manga' means 'comic books'. In the English-speaking world, manga is used as a general term for all comic books and graphic novels that come from Japan.

Manga comic books first became popular when a magazine called *Hokusai Manga* was published. It had drawings by a famous Japanese artist called Hokusai, who had developed a style of drawing called ukiyo-e. Later, the ukiyo-e style was mixed with Western drawing and this formed the style of drawing we call manga today.

Making Manga

A manga author or artist is called mangaka. While each mangaka has his or her own style, there are some drawing techniques that give manga its unique look. For example, most characters have large, round or almond-shaped eyes. Mangakas pay special attention to how they draw their characters' eyes, as these are the main features which show what the character is thinking and feeling. A manga character will usually have a simple nose and mouth. A mouth is usually small when closed and big when opened.

Signs of Emotion

Manga drawings have certain signs that show a particular emotion. For example, a sweat drop on the forehead shows 'worry'. The same signs are used in all manga drawings so that the reader gets to know what the sign stands for. This helps the reader to know what the character is thinking and feeling.

Eyes Right

The most outstanding feature of typical manga characters is their large, saucer-sized eyes. In fact, some manga artists start their work with the eyes, because they are the most important feature in creating the look and 'feel' of the character. Manga characters display a wide range of emotions with their eyes, from happiness and joy, to seething anger and deep sadness. Large eyes are also used to show that a character is friendly and honest – the good guy! Small eyes usually show a nasty and cold character, lacking in emotion and with evil thoughts – the bad guy!

Get Drawing

In this book we will show you how to draw the Fantasy Fighters in manga style. These intergalactic warriors travel through time and space to protect the universe from evil forces. Have fun!

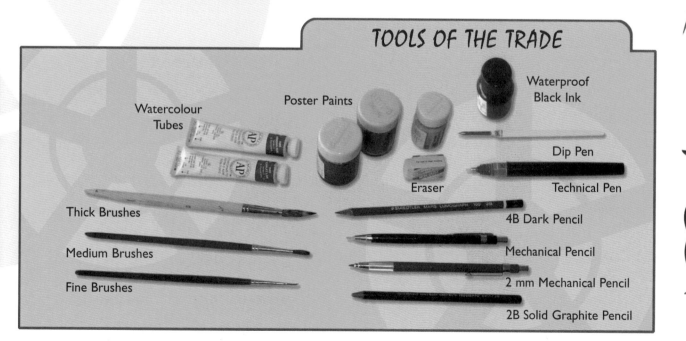

TOOLS OF THE TRADE

Watercolour Tubes

Poster Paints

Waterproof Black Ink

Dip Pen

Technical Pen

Eraser

Thick Brushes

4B Dark Pencil

Medium Brushes

Mechanical Pencil

Fine Brushes

2 mm Mechanical Pencil

2B Solid Graphite Pencil

FIGURE DRAWING

It is very important for a manga artist to understand how to draw the human body. Start by making a simple standing figure, as shown here.

Male and Female Proportions

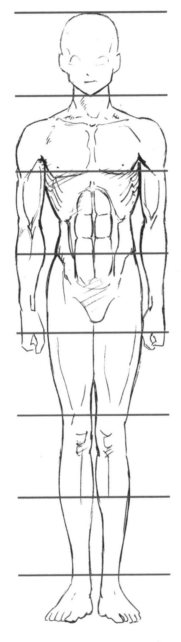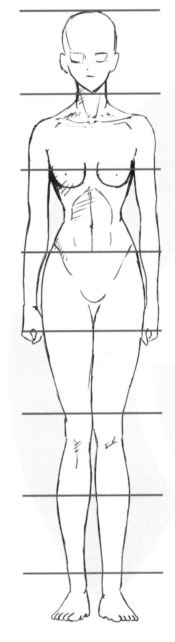

The human figure is measured in 'heads' to get the proportions right. As shown above, the body is divided into seven and a half 'heads' (each section is equivalent to the length of an adult head).

Female hips are wider than their shoulders. For men it is the opposite and the shoulders are wider than the hips. The female figure is slimmer than the male body because it has less muscle.

Turn to the next page to see how the character is
developed further and then completed.
Do the steps below first though.

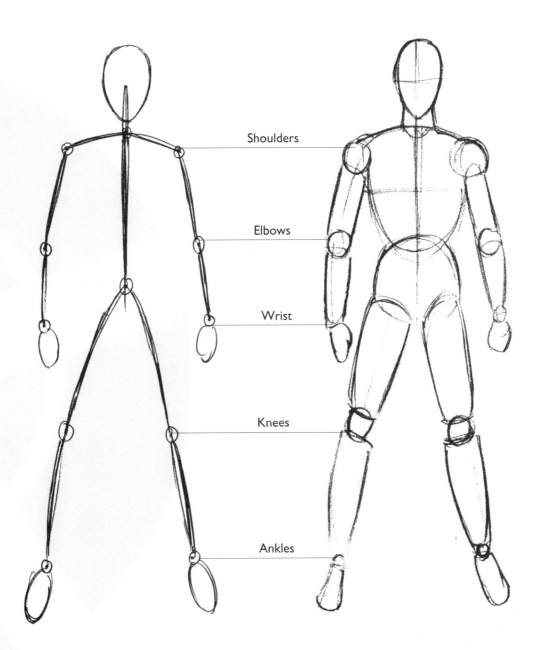

Shoulders

Elbows

Wrist

Knees

Ankles

Draw a straight line for the
spine. Add more lines to draw a
complete stick figure. Add small
circles, or dots, to show where
the joints of the body are, as
shown above.

Finally, add bigger circles to show
the head, hands and feet. Now, add
bulk to the body to show its size.
Use curved lines and circles to
show the size of the arms and legs,
and top and bottom of the torso.

CHARACTER POSES

Practise drawing the human figure. Once you have the basic proportions right, add final details to make your drawing look like a real character. Then try drawing different poses. Look carefully at the poses here and in manga comics. Copy the figures to get a feel for different 'action' positions.

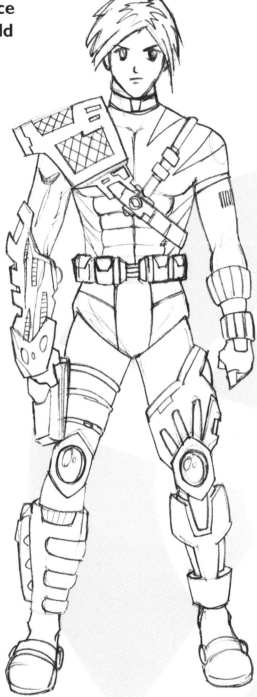

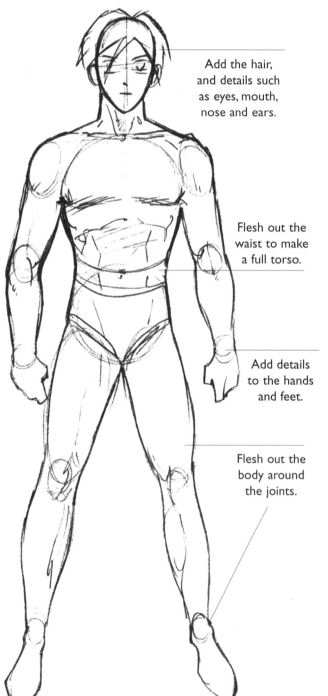

Add the hair, and details such as eyes, mouth, nose and ears.

Flesh out the waist to make a full torso.

Add details to the hands and feet.

Flesh out the body around the joints.

Finally, when you have finished your basic figure, rub out the guidelines and add the clothes.

Here are some action poses. Can you imagine what the stick figure might look like? Try drawing it ... then flesh out the figure.

THE EYE

The eyes are one of the most recognisable features of manga drawing. They are usually wide and round to show innocence. Baddies usually have narrower eyes. Look carefully at the eyes and eyebrows of different manga characters to see how the eyes are drawn to show what the individual character is like.

Basic Eye

First draw a circle for the eye. Add two more inside it for the pupil and the iris.

Next draw the upper eyelid. It should overlap the eyeball at the top.

Similarly, draw the lower eyelid to complete the basic eye.

Manga Eye

Use a curved, light stroke to sketch the basic shape of the upper and lower lid.

Now draw in an oval for the eyeball.

Sketch out the upper eyelid and fold lines. Use a dark pencil to mark out the top eyelid line.

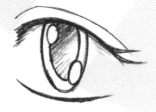

Add a circle on the upper edge of the eyeball for the highlight or white spot.

Add an oval within the eyeball to make the pupil. Add solid lines for the eyelashes. Add a second highlight circle.

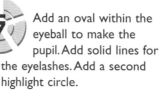

When the eye is finished, rub out the guidelines. Shade in the pupil using a dark pencil.

Types of Manga Eye

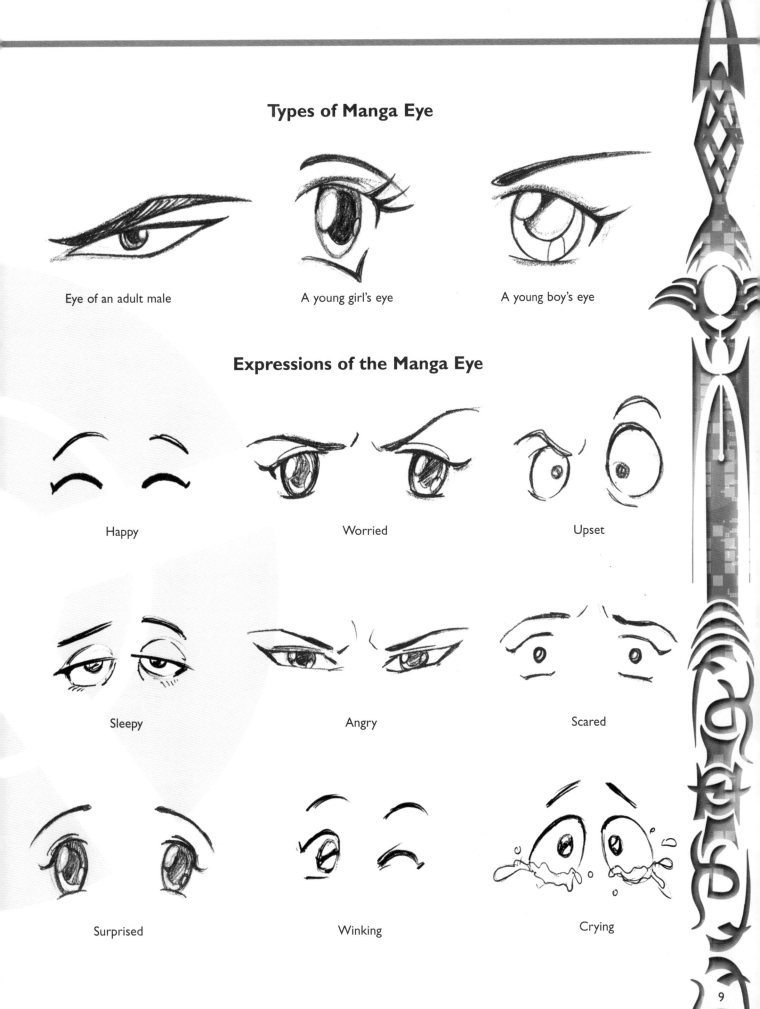

Eye of an adult male

A young girl's eye

A young boy's eye

Expressions of the Manga Eye

Happy

Worried

Upset

Sleepy

Angry

Scared

Surprised

Winking

Crying

MANGA HEAD

Follow the steps shown here to learn how to draw a manga head. Once you have learnt the basic rules, you can add lots of different features, such as hairstyles, helmets, caps, goggles and glasses.

Front View

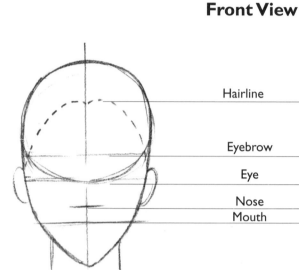

Hairline

Eyebrow

Eye

Nose

Mouth

1 Draw an oval shape and divide it into four by making a '+' mark through it. Now, mark the position of the eyes, nose and mouth using the cross as a guide. Sketch in the ears and the neck.

2 Roughly sketch the eyes and eyebrows. The distance between the eyes should be the length of one eye. Mark the hairline and sketch in the hair. Define the ears and add detail to flesh them out.

3 Draw in the eyes – see pages 8-9. The eyebrows should be a solid shape. Use a small tick mark to draw in the nose.

4 Draw a simple mouth with a couple of lines. The mouth should be about as wide as one eye. Finish the hairstyle and rub out the guidelines.

Side View

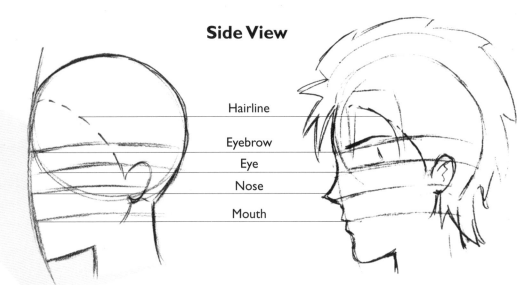

Hairline

Eyebrow

Eye

Nose

Mouth

1 Draw an oval shape for the head. It should be pointed on one side for the chin. Make a line to mark the position of the eye about halfway down the head. Make a line for the nose halfway between the eye and the chin. Make a line for the mouth halfway between the nose and the chin.

2 Add the ear near the back of the head, in line with the nose. Pencil in the hairline and add the rough hairstyle. Draw the shape of the nose and lips. Add the eyebrow.

3 Draw in the eye. It should be about one eye width in from the edge of the front of the face. Add a little shading to the nostrils to finish the nose.

4 Add finishing touches to the eye and ear. Add a line to finish the mouth. Finally, complete the hairstyle and rub out the guidelines.

THE HAND

Many people think that hands are difficult to draw, but like the rest of the body, they are just shapes put together. Start with a stick figure hand and gradually flesh it out. Look at pictures of hands, especially manga hands ... take notice of how they are used.

1. Make a hand by drawing a box. Sketch in five lines for the fingers and the thumb. Mark the knuckles with small circles.

2. Now flesh out the sketch by drawing tubes for each finger. Remember to keep the knuckles in a curve and not in a straight line.

3. Use a fine pencil to add more details, such as the nails and finger knuckles or joints.

TOP TIPS

Do not use straight lines when drawing hands. Using curved lines will make your hands look more real.

Incorrect

Correct

Look at your own hands in different positions.
Think about the shapes they make then
draw the shapes. Keep practising.

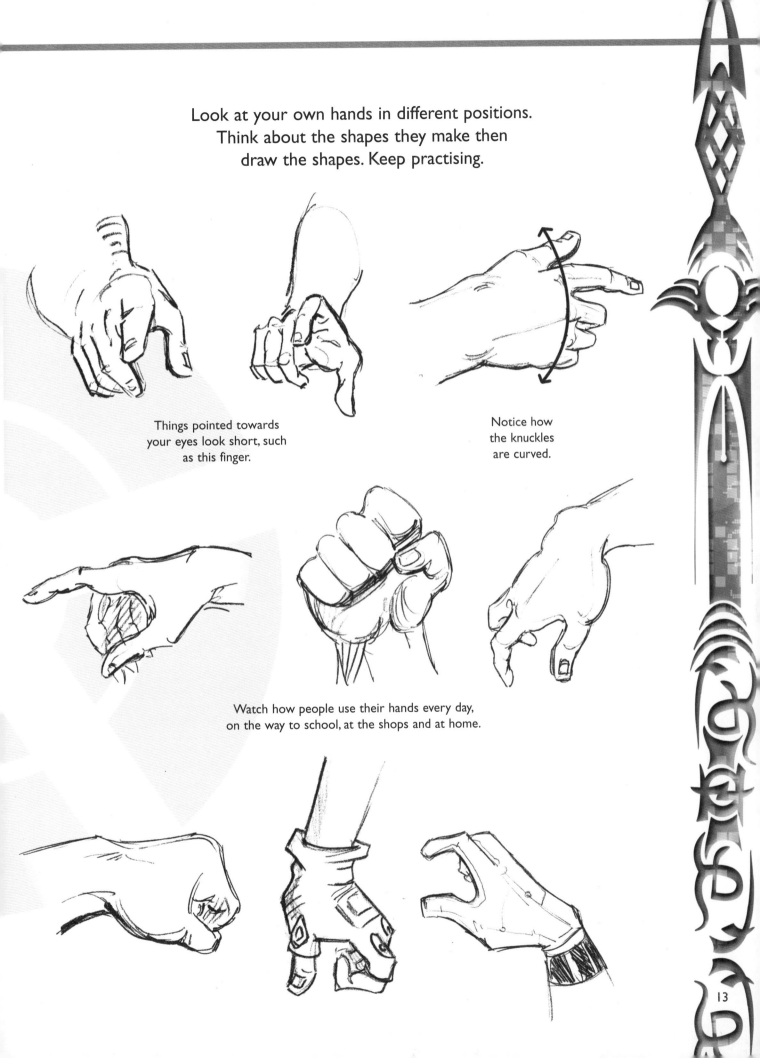

Things pointed towards
your eyes look short, such
as this finger.

Notice how
the knuckles
are curved.

Watch how people use their hands every day,
on the way to school, at the shops and at home.

THE FOOT

Let's learn more about how to draw some of the individual parts of the body. Here is a simple step-by-step guide to drawing the basic foot.

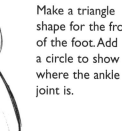

Make a triangle shape for the front of the foot. Add a circle to show where the ankle joint is.

Draw lines for toes

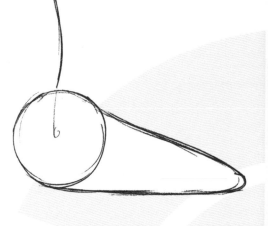

For a side view of the foot, draw a circle and attach a triangle to it like this.

To draw toes, create 5 curved, tube shapes. Remember each toe is a different size. Add the leg.

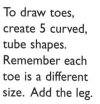

Add circles for toenails

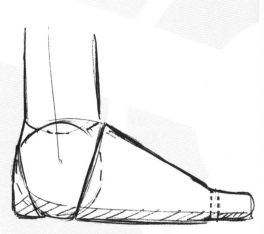

Flesh out the foot. Add a toe shape at the end of the triangle. Add shape to the heel. Add the leg.

Using a fine pencil, add final shape and details to the foot. Use a thicker pencil to add some shade.

With a thicker pencil, shade in the ankle bone and draw in the toenail.

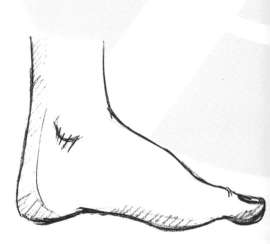

Look at pictures of feet at different angles. You can illustrate details like the ankles by adding light and shade.

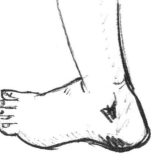

Tiptoe

Left foot

Here we have put fantasy shoes on the bare feet. Think about the shapes that have been used to make the footwear. Draw some shoes of your own.

A warrior princess's shoe

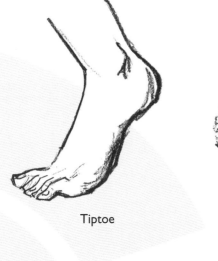

Inner side of the left foot

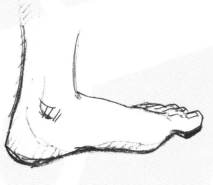

Front of the foot

TOP TIPS

Light Shading   Dark Shading

Use fine pencil lines to add details to the feet, such as the ankle bone. Use a thicker pencil to draw in toenails.

Add thick and thin pencil lines for shading.

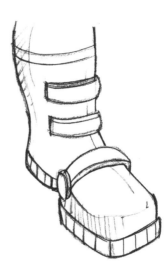

This tough shoe is for the battles on a rough surface.

EXPRESSIONS

A variety of expressions can be shown on a manga face by simply changing the eyes, eyebrows and mouth. These features can be drawn to show a wide range of emotions. Below are some basic ways to show different expressions.

A gaping mouth with wide eyes and slanting eyebrows drawn in a frown shows rage. The wide open mouth has him yelling loudly.

Slanting the eyebrows upwards is the easiest way to show surprise. The rounded eyes and mouth help to create a stronger effect.

Closed eyes are drawn in two ways – curved upwards or downwards. Curving upwards with a smiling mouth is often used to show happiness.

Here the outer corners of the eyebrows slant up and join the eyes, and the eyes are very narrow. This shows quiet anger or that the character is in deep thought.

Here, the downward arch of the eye shows the character is thinking about something. It is made stronger by the slight downturn of the eyebrows and the downwards curve of the mouth.

The expressions of shock and surprise are similar. However, in shock, the eyes are not so rounded – just opened wide. The gaping mouth adds to the overall effect.

The slight upwards arch of the eyebrows is often used to show calmness or happiness. It can also show a character having happy memories or thoughts.

The slyness of this character is shown by the upside down 'v' shape of the eyebrows. The slightly slanted slits of the eyes and the mouth tilting at the corner make the expression stronger.

XEN OF ZEUS

Xen is a state-of-the-art fighting machine from a future time and place who travels backwards and forwards through time. He's a cyborg living in a human body and comes from a warrior clan from the planet Zeus!

1. Draw a stick figure with the head, body, arms and legs in the action position. Make ovals to show the joints of the body and the position of the hands and feet.

2. Now draw curved lines to flesh out the body. Look at the finished picture and think about the shape of the body under the clothes.

3. Next, sketch the hair and the outline of the clothing and add weapons and other accessories. Don't forget to draw in Xen's favourite weapon – the pulsar gun!

4. Finally, add detail to the face, hands and feet, and complete the look of the character. Draw his blaster gun with his other weapon, his sword. When you have finished, rub out guidelines.

5. Now comes the fun part – colour in your drawing. Here he is wearing red and yellow but you can add your own combination of bright colours. Now that he is fully equipped, Xen is ready to fight!

TENCHU

Tenchu is a brave warrior from the planet Izzak. His mission in life is to defend the powerless and wipe out all evil from his world. The pulsar pistols he carries can turn any living or non-living thing into dust. Tenchu prefers to fight on land, but can put up a mean fight in space, and even in water if necessary.

1. First, draw a stick figure. Think about how the move will affect his back. In this pose, the spine is curved. Draw small ovals to show the joints of the body. Add shapes for the hands and feet.

2. Now draw curved lines to flesh out the body. Look at the finished picture and think about what the body looks like before all the clothes and accessories are added.

3. Next, add hair. Sketch the outline of Tenchu's clothes and weapons and other accessories. Tenchu loves his pulsar pistols. Don't forget to draw them in. He would be lost without them!

4 Finally, add details to the face, hands and feet, and complete the look of the character. Don't forget to rub out the guidelines. Add his pulsar pistols and he's ready for combat!

5 Colour your drawing using the right flesh tones. You can choose any of your favourite colours for the clothes. Wow, look at Tenchu! He seems ready for a good fight!

SHYNE

Shyne was born with amazing powers, but no-one knows where they came from. Some believe that she is an incarnation of Galemma, the Witch Goddess. Shyne, however, believes her powers are a gift from her parents, who used to practise white magic. Shyne can fly, as well as send out energy blasts. She can also read minds and control objects with her psychic powers.

1. First, draw a stick figure. Draw ovals to show the joints of the body and the hands and feet.

2. Now draw curved lines to flesh out the body. Look at the finished picture and think about what the body looks like before all the clothes and accessories are added.

3. Next, add her hair. Then sketch the outline of Shyne's clothes and add weapons and other accessories. Outline her facial features. Note the shape of her ears.

4 Finally, add detail to the face, hands and feet, and complete the look of the character. Don't forget to rub out the guidelines. Add her telekinesis head gear which controls and enhances her power.

5 Next, colour your drawing using the right flesh tones. As Shyne is a witch, you might want to use different shades of blue for her clothes.

NEO

Neo is a natural acrobat and fighter. He is from the planet F'shun where all warriors make their living fighting with each other. Neo rose from the streets to become the leader of his gang, NeoGeo. He has no super powers, but with his strength and fighting skills he can make even the most powerful enemy beg for mercy!

1. First, draw a stick figure. Draw ovals to show the joints of the body and hands and feet.

2. Now draw curved lines to flesh out the body. Look at the finished picture and think about what the body looks like before all the clothes and accessories are added.

3. Next, sketch the outline of Neo's clothes and add weapons and other accessories. Remember, Neo is a fighter with no super powers, so you will have to arm him properly.

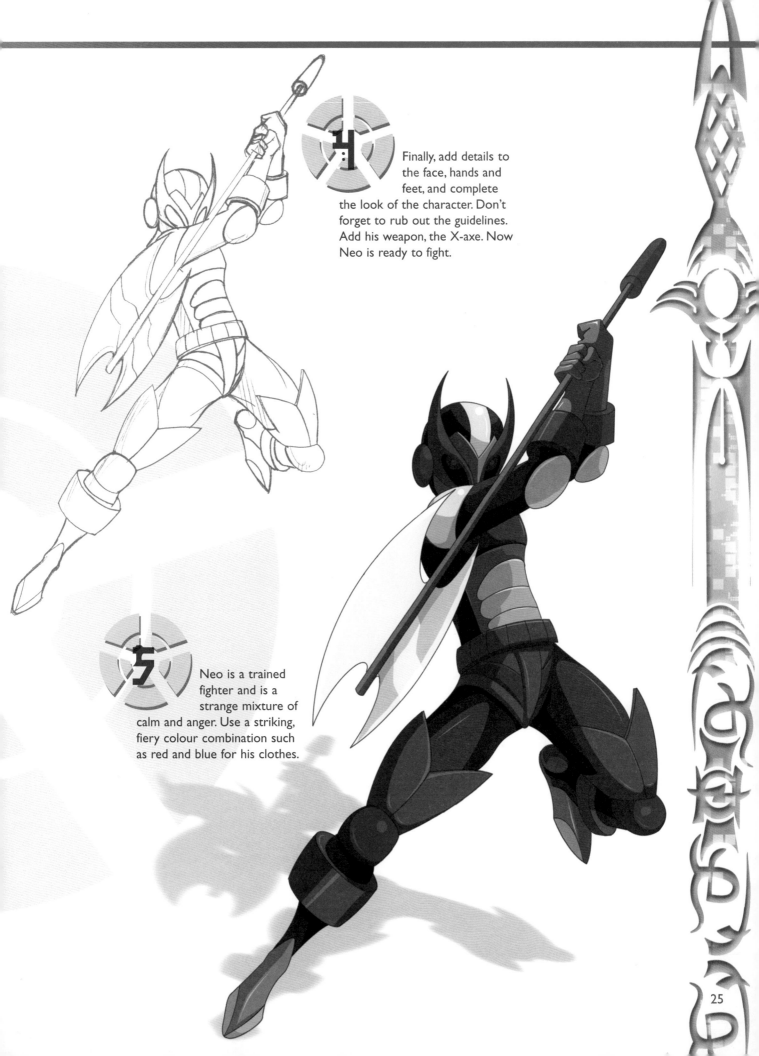

4 Finally, add details to the face, hands and feet, and complete the look of the character. Don't forget to rub out the guidelines. Add his weapon, the X-axe. Now Neo is ready to fight.

5 Neo is a trained fighter and is a strange mixture of calm and anger. Use a striking, fiery colour combination such as red and blue for his clothes.

SPROKET

Sproket is a young rocketeer who lives life dangerously. His dad was a scientist and gave him a jet pack when he was a little boy. Now that he is grown up, he has a highly advanced spacesuit to go with the jet pack. With his hi-fi gear, Sproket can fly through the universe to make it a better place. He can shoot energy bolts and fly faster than a bullet.

1. First, draw a stick figure. Draw ovals to indicate the joints of the body and the hands and feet.

2. Now draw curved lines to flesh out the body. Look at the finished picture and think about what the body looks like before all the clothes and accessories are added.

3. Next, sketch the outline of the clothes and add his helmet, weapons and other accessories. Sproket's strength lies in his jet pack, so don't forget to add that.

Jet pack

4 Finally, add details to the face, hands and feet, and complete the look of the character. Don't forget to rub out the guidelines. Finish his helmet, arm bands and booster shoes and Sproket is now ready to fly away.

5 Colouring Sproket is fun. Use flesh tones for his body, but use your imagination to colour in his clothes. Mix and match is the theme for this rocketeer!

GARETT

Garett is the last warrior of his clan, which belongs to an unknown planet. Garett is half-alien and half-elf, and has the power to control objects with his mind. He is also a trained fighter. His favourite weapon is the twin blade, made from alien technology not known to many, but beware of his hypnotic eye! No fighter in the universe dare look straight into that deadly weapon!

1. First, draw a stick figure, keeping the head, body, arms and legs in the right position. Draw ovals to show the joints of the body and the hands and feet.

2. Now draw curved lines to flesh out the body. Look at the finished picture and think about what the body looks like before all the clothes and accessories are added.

3. Next, add the hair. Sketch the outline of the clothes and add weapons and other accessories. In this case, draw in Garett's favourite weapon, his twin blade.

Finally, add details to the face, hands and feet, and complete the look of the character. Add his hypnotic eye. The round part should be the same size as his real eye and just slightly lower. Don't make the rest of it too big.

Colour your drawing using the correct flesh tones. However, why not try different colours for Garett's hair? And add light and shade to his hypnotic eye to make it gleam!

29

TARR

Tarr is a one-man army – actually he's half-man and half-elf. His precious bow and arrows can shoot any object no matter how far away. Tarr never misses a target. His arrows are made up of various metals and have different powers – there are electric arrows, tornado arrows, spike-bomb arrows, missile arrows and nerve arrows, to name just a few.

1. First, draw a stick figure keeping the head, body, arms and legs in the right position. Draw ovals to show the joints of the body and the hands and feet.

2. Now draw curved lines to flesh out the body. Look at the finished picture and think about what the body looks like before all the clothes and accessories are added.

3. Next, add the hair and his pointed ears. Sketch the outline of the clothes and add weapons and other accessories. Choose an arrow from Tarr's quiver to put in his bow.

4

Finally, add details to the face, hands and feet, and finish the look of the character. Rub out the guidelines when you have finished. Add detail to his steel bow and its arrow, and Tarr is ready to meet any enemy.

5

Colouring Tarr can be quite a challenge. As he's only half-human, you don't need to stick to the usual colours for his body or hair. Use cool colours for his clothes and accessories.

YOSHI

Yoshi is a rich businessman by day and a notorious robber by night. This thief steals from everyone. He can also make himself invisible to the naked eye. Yoshi is not much of a fighter, but makes up for this with his cleverness and cunning. He loves gold and diamond jewellery and valuable art objects.

1. First, draw a stick figure keeping the head, body, arms and legs in the right position. Draw ovals to show the joints of the body and the hands and feet.

2. Now draw curved lines to flesh out the body. Look at the finished picture and think about what the body looks like before all the clothes and accessories are added.

3. Next, add hair. Sketch the outline of Yoshi's clothes and add other accessories. Remember, in this case there aren't any weapons. Yoshi's power lies in his super brain.

4 Finally, add details to the face, hands and feet, and complete the look of the character. Rub out the guidelines when you have finished. Add his mask, his mechanical arm and details to his anti-pressure fastening shoes. Now he's ready to go!

5 Colour your drawing using the right flesh tones. Use light shades for the clothes. Try not to use too many bright colours as Yoshi does not want to stand out in a crowd.

KRIKON

Krikon has an IQ ten times greater than a normal human. He travels through space, keeping the peace between all the planets. Krikon's peace mission was given to him by an alien he saved when its spaceship crash-landed on Earth. Krikon's powers and the suit he wears are all part of a technology unknown to humans. His main weapons are his two 'takostiks', which are powered by alien energy.

1. First, draw a stick figure keeping the head, body, arms and legs in the right position. Draw ovals to show the joints of the body and the hands and feet.

2. Now draw curved lines to flesh out the body. Look at the finished picture and think about what the body looks like before all the clothes and accessories are added.

3. Next, sketch the outline of the clothes and add weapons and other accessories. Takostiks filled with alien energy are the main weapons of this super-scientist.

Finally, add details to the face, hands and feet, and complete the look of the character. Rub out the guidelines when you have finished. Complete his takostiks, his powerful weapons, and don't forget to show some energy blasting out of them!

Colour your drawing using the right flesh tones. Combine shades of grey, blue and bright pink to make Krikon's clothes cool and colourful.

MEDUSA

Medusa is a secret agent who is both sly and cunning. She knows every fighting style there is to know. She can fight with her bare hands or with any weapon. As an orphan, Medusa was adopted and trained by an agency to become one of the greatest soldiers ever. Medusa has no special weapon, but loves the powerful 'sis-guns' designed just for her.

1. First, draw a stick figure keeping the head, body, arms and legs in the right position. Draw ovals to show the joints of the body and the hands and feet.

2. Now draw curved lines to flesh out the body. Look at the finished picture and think about what the body looks like before all the clothes and accessories are added.

3. Next, add her cap and hair. Sketch the outline of Medusa's clothes and add weapons and other accessories. Remember, Medusa never leaves home without her sis-guns!

4: Finally, add details to the face, hands and feet, and complete the look of the character. Rub out the guidelines when you have finished. Finalise the detail on her powerful sis-guns so she's ready for action!

5: Colour your drawing using the right flesh tones. Medusa is full of energy, so give her bright, colourful clothes. Make her guns a matching colour and notice the shading on them.

ENJILL

Enjill is an alien from an unknown planet who was brought up on Earth. Enjill looks human but works for an alien agency. She can grow wings and has been trained to fight with different weapons. With her cat-like eyes, Enjill is able to see in total darkness. She enjoys using big, heavy guns and has no trouble fighting with them.

1. First, draw a stick figure keeping the head, body, arms and legs in the right position. Draw ovals to show the joints of the body and the hands and feet.

2. Now draw curved lines to flesh out the body. Look at the finished picture and think about what the body looks like before all the clothes and accessories are added.

3. Next, sketch the outline of the clothes and add weapons and other accessories. Don't forget her wings and helmet!

4 Finally, add details to the face, hands and feet, and complete the look of the character. Rub out the guidelines when you have finished. Complete her wing blades, goggles, helmet and gun, so she's ready to fly at the first sign of trouble!

5 Enjill might be an alien but she doesn't want to give that secret away! So use normal flesh tones for her skin. But you can choose any of your favourite colours for her clothes.

NADYA

Nadya is an ancient warrior who has been travelling through time. Her lone mission is to solve her father's mysterious death. Nadya belongs to a world of white magic and sorcery. But she doesn't use magic for fighting. Her favourite weapon is the nanchuk blades, which her father gave to her before he died.

1. First, draw a stick figure keeping the head, body, arms and legs in the right position. Draw circles to show the joints of the body and the hands and feet.

2. Now draw curved lines to flesh out the body. Look at the finished picture and think about what the body looks like before all the clothes and accessories are added.

3. Next, add her hair. Then sketch the outline of her clothes and add weapons and other accessories. Remember, Nadya can't do without the nanchuk blades her father gave her.

4 Finally, add details to the face, hands and feet, and complete the look of the character. Rub out the guidelines when you have finished. Nadya has a fierce expression. Her mouth should curve down slightly at the sides and her eyebrows are frowning.

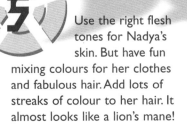

5 Use the right flesh tones for Nadya's skin. But have fun mixing colours for her clothes and fabulous hair. Add lots of streaks of colour to her hair. It almost looks like a lion's mane!

COLOURING TECHNIQUES

Now that you have learnt how to draw the characters, let's look at the various effects you can achieve using different colouring techniques.

Use a pencil to add light and dark shade to the picture. Use very fine strokes to begin with. Make the pencilwork darker by adding more strokes on top. For white highlights, use an eraser to rub out the pencil so the white of the paper shows through.

You can build up shading using a technique called 'wash'. Mix black ink or paint with water to make a thin colour or 'wash'. Brush this on the area you want to colour. Let it dry. Mix more black paint with water and put this where you want the picture to be darker. Always leave the paper to dry before you add the next layer.

You can use coloured pencils to make light and dark areas using the same technique as for the black pencil above. To make the highlights, leave the paper blank or rub out the pencil.

You can add colour using the same wash technique as above. Choose a colour, such as blue, and mix with water. Do a very light wash first and brush it on the area you want to colour. Build up the colour gradually.

You can paint straight onto the
paper using poster paint colours.
You can mix poster paint with
water to make the colour lighter.
For the highlights, add white paint
using a very fine brush.

This image has been coloured
digitally on the computer. Some
manga artists colour in this way
but many still colour in by hand.

SHADING FIGURES

You can change the look of your Fantasy Fighter dramatically by simply adding a light source. Adding shades of light and dark can change the depth and mood of the figure, and help to make it appear more lifelike. Let's experiment by adding a light source from different angles to the same figure.

From the Right
In this picture, the light source is coming from the right of the figure. This makes the shadow fall on the left part of the arms, legs and body.

From the Top

When the light source comes from the top of the figure, the shadow falls straight down. You can see the shadow under the hair, nose and neck.

From the Left

Here, the light source is coming from the left of the figure. The shadow falls near the right part of the nose and hands, and the right side of the body.

COMBAT GEAR

At last, time to put the finishing touches your Fantasy Fighter! Here is a range of accessories and weapons to choose from to make your Fantasy Fighter really spectacular!

Chest Armour
This protects the fighter from heat, cold, bullets, fire blasts and attack from any weapon or force.

Futuristic Eyepiece
This helps the warrior to focus on a target during a battle. It is a high-powered binocular and microscope, all in one. Some of its special features include x-ray vision, night vision and infra-red heat sensors.

Pulsar Gun
Each energy bolt has 15,000 watts. This gun can blow all known metals to smithereens.

Dragon Gauntlet
This can carry the heaviest object.

Dragon Sword
The heaviest and most powerful sword of all. It can cut through any metal known to man.

Fantasy Fighter Headgear

Mechanical Eye
This acts like a third eye for the fighter, and helps him or her to spy on enemy hideouts and fight in stealth mode.

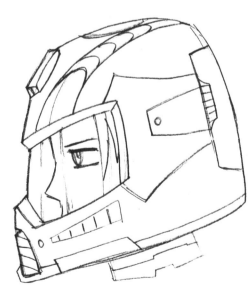

Mask
This protects the fighter's face from harmful gases and keeps his or her real identity a secret.

Helmet
This all-purpose headgear not only gives protection to the fighter's head, but also helps him or her when travelling through time or moving from one dimension to another.

CLASSIC POSES

Let's take a look at some of the classic poses of your favourite Fantasy Fighters.

With that powerful jet-pack suit of his, this fast runner can even beat lightning!

This is a futuristic ninja. Stealth fighting is his skill, and naturally he is very acrobatic.

She is a witch who uses her powers for the good of the universe. She flies using her magical staff.

She is a powerful princess who will fight an enemy with any weapon she can lay her hands on.